Young
Harriet Tubman

Freedom Fighter

A Troll First-Start® Biography

by Anne Benjamin
illustrated by Ellen Beier

Troll Associates

Library of Congress Cataloging-in-Publication Data

Benjamin, Anne.
    Young Harriet Tubman: freedom fighter / by Anne Benjamin;
illustrated by Ellen Beier.
        p.   cm.—(First-start biographies)
    Summary: A simple biography of the black woman who helped over 300
slaves escape through the Underground Railroad and was never caught
herself.
    ISBN 0-8167-2538-1 (lib. bdg.)   ISBN 0-8167-2539-X (pbk.)
    1. Tubman, Harriet, 1820?-1913—Juvenile literature.   2. Slaves—
United States—Biography—Juvenile literature.   3. Afro-Americans—
Biography—Juvenile literature.   4. Underground railroad—Juvenile
literature. [1. Tubman, Harriet, 1820?-1913.   2. Slaves.   3. Afro-
Americans—Biography.   4. Underground railroad.] I. Beier, Ellen,
ill. II. Title. III. Series.
E444.T82B43   1992
305.5'67'092—dc20
[B]   91-26404

Harriet Ross Tubman was born a slave. But she spent her whole life fighting for freedom.

3

There are no slaves in America now.
But when Harriet was born, around
1820, slaves worked on big Southern
farms called plantations. They worked
in the hot sun from dawn to dusk.
It was hard, terrible work.

Harriet and her family belonged to a
farmer named Edward Brodas. They
lived in a one-room shack on his
land. It had no windows or furniture.
Harriet and her family slept on rags
on the dirt floor.

Harriet was only 3 when she started working. Even though she was just a little girl, she had to carry messages many miles for Mr. Brodas.

She was also hired out to work for
other families. Sometimes they were
very cruel to her.

When she was 9 years old, Harriet
cleaned houses and took care of babies.
It was hard work for a little girl.

Harriet did not complain. She did not want Mr. Brodas to sell her to another master. Two of her sisters had been sold already.

After dark, the slaves got together to talk about freedom. They told stories about Moses, the man who led his people out of slavery. And they spoke about the underground railroad, which took slaves to freedom in the north.

The underground railroad was not
really a train. It was a group of
people, both blacks and whites, who
felt slavery was wrong. Some people
hid slaves in their homes. Others
led slaves from one "station," or
house, to the next.

15

Harriet loved to listen to these stories.
One day, she promised herself,
she would take the underground
railroad to freedom.

But Harriet almost didn't get her
chance. At the age of 15, she was
in a store when a slave and his
master ran in.

The master told his slave to get back
to work. The slave refused. His master
was so angry, he threw a heavy iron
weight at him. But the weight hit
Harriet in the head instead.

19

Harriet was sick for many months. She almost died. And she had a terrible scar on her forehead for the rest of her life.

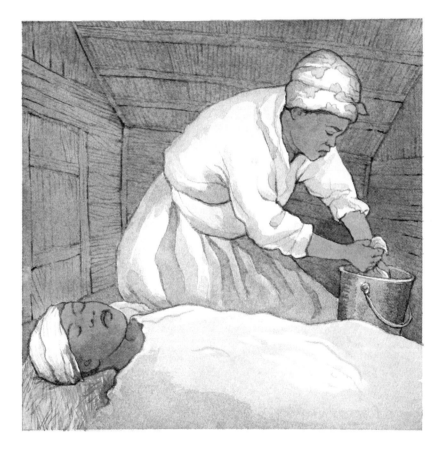

In time, Harriet went back to work.
But now she wanted her freedom more
than ever.

Finally, in 1849, Harriet heard that Mr. Brodas was going to sell many of his slaves. She knew the time had come to run away.

During the day, Harriet hid in people's houses. She knew Mr. Brodas was looking for her.

At night, she walked for miles through the woods to get to the next station on the underground railroad. The journey north was long and dangerous. But there were many people to help her on her way.

At last Harriet reached Pennsylvania.
There was no slavery there.
Harriet was free!

Harriet could not forget that her
family was still in slavery. She went
back and brought them to freedom,
too. But there were many more people
who needed her help.

Harriet helped over 300 slaves escape on the underground railroad. The slaves called her Moses. They loved this brave woman very much.

The slave-owners hated her!
They offered a $40,000 reward for
Harriet's capture. But Harriet was
never caught.

During the Civil War, Harriet worked as a spy for the Northern army. She helped many more slaves escape to freedom.

Even after slavery ended, Harriet kept
on helping people. She spoke out for
women's rights. She started schools
for black children and homes for
poor black families.

When Harriet died at 93, she was given a military funeral. It was a great honor for the woman who had fought so hard for freedom.